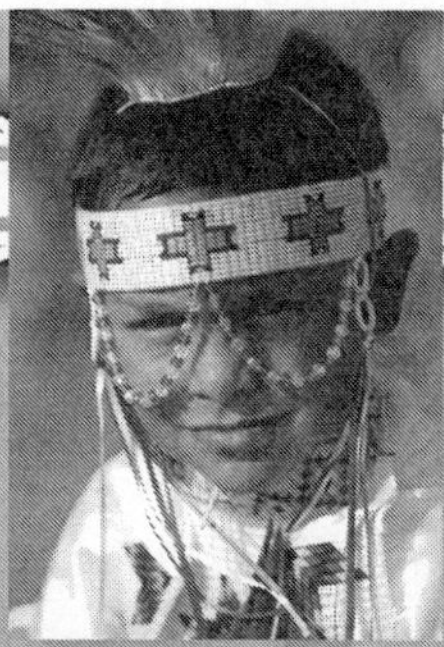

Kansas Native Americans

A Kid's Look at Our State's Chiefs, Tribes, Reservations, Powwows, Lore, and More From The Past and the Present

By Carole Marsh

Native American Heritage™

Graphic Design: Lynette Rowe • Cover Design: Victoria DeJoy

Published by
GALLOPADE INTERNATIONAL
800-536-2GET
www.gallopade.com

Gallopade is proud to be a member of these educational organizations and associations:

The National School Supply and Equipment Association (NSSEA)
American Booksellers Association (ABA)
Virginia Educational Media Association (VEMA)
Association of Partners for Public Lands (APPL)
Museum Store Association (MSA)
National Association for Gifted Children (NAGC)
Publishers Marketing Association (PMA)
International Reading Association (IRA)
Association of African American Museums (AAAM)

Native American Heritage™ Series

Native American Big Activity Book

Native American Biographies

Native American Coloring Book

Native American Heritage Book

Native American Timeline

Kansas State Stuff™

- My First Pocket Guide: Kansas
- My First Book About Kansas
- Kansas Coloring Book
- The Big Kansas Reproducible Activity Book
- Jeopardy: Answers & Questions About Our State
- Kansas "Jography!": A Fun Run Through Our State
- Kansas Gamebooks
- Kansas Bingo Games
- Kansas Illustrated Timelines
- Kansas Project Books
- Kansas Bulletin Board Set
- Kansas PosterMap
- Kansas Stickers
- Let's Discover Kansas! CD-ROM

Word from the Author

Hello!

I hope you are as interested in North America's wonderful Indian heritage as I am!

Like most kids, I grew up thinking of Indians as the other half of Cowboys. Today, of course, we are getting a much clearer and more accurate picture of what the first peoples on our land were all about. These "facts" are much more fascinating than anything Hollywood can make up. And you probably won't find much of this information in your history textbook!

I am 1/16 Cherokee. This is something I am very proud of and happy about. My grandmother was 1/4 Cherokee. She had tan skin, long gray hair and a very Indian look – especially if I did something bad! Her maiden name was Carrie Corn. Of course, when she got married, she took her husband's name, so it was many years before I learned to appreciate the significance of my native heritage.

Today, I'm trying to make up for lost time by exploring my roots as deeply as I can. One of the most interesting things I've learned is how fascinating all of the Indian tribes are – in the past, the present and future!

As you read about "your" Indians, remember that all native peoples were part of an ever-changing network of time, ideas, power and luck — good and bad. This is certainly a history that is not "dead," but continues to change – often right outside our own back doors! – all the time.

Carole Marsh
She-Who-Writes

PS: Many references show different spellings for the same word. I have tried to select the most common spelling for the time period described. I would not want to be in an Indian spelling bee!

A is for . . .

Antelope

Used as food and clothing by Kansas Indians. Buckskin was used for moccasin tops and vests, hair for pillow and mattress stuffing, shinbones for pipes and horns for tools.

Awl

An Indian's "needle." Often made from wood, thorns, bone, or metal, it was used to punch holes in skins so they could be sewn together.

Adze

An Indian woodworking tool used to cut, scrape, or gouge; often used to hollow dugout canoes. Blades were made of stone, shell, bone or copper.

Apache

Nomadic tribe, known as fierce raiders and warriors. Roamed into southern Kansas. When they couldn't find enough food, they raided other tribes or settlements for it. Master basketmakers. Had a hard time adapting to the confinement of reservation life, and accepting the government's banning of some religious practices.

Agriculture

Early Kansas Indians slowly learned to farm. Corn or maize was a staple crop. They used tools like stone axes to clear trees and bowls to grind corn.

Altar

A platform made of rocks or animal skulls; some had bowls, feathers, rattles, or skins on them. Indians prayed at these altars for things like good crops or expert hunting skills.

Arrow

A long, slender shaft made of reed, cane, or wood; pointed tip was attached to one end and split feathers to the other. Feathers helped the arrows fly straight.

Adobe

Brick made of mud plus straw and dried in the sun. Houses made of adobe are cool inside, even in high temperatures, because the walls are so thick.

Aborigine

A member of the earliest known population of a region.

Arrowhead

The pointed tip of an arrow, made of bone, antler, wood, or iron. Some tips had barbs that would embed themselves in flesh. These barbs made it difficult for an enemy to remove the arrowhead from a wound.

B is for . . .

Bonner Springs

Site of a 1988 archaeological find of early Indian bones, one fragment older than any other previously found in the New World. Pottery shards, grindstones and flint knives were also unearthed at the site. These discoveries proved that people lived in Kansas as early as 15,000 years ago.

Band

A subdivision of an Indian tribe. In earlier times, a band was sometimes created when part of a tribe split off from the main group. The band also chose new leadership.

Blankets

Used for door covers, partitions, bags, to dry food on, carry babies and many other purposes.

Baskets

Some were woven and others were coiled. Baskets were made from roots, grasses, barks, and other natural materials.

Buffalo

Made up the major diet of many Indian tribes. Hides were used as blankets or tents. Every tribe member was given a piece of the animal to eat. There were strict rules about not hunting buffalo alone, so that one person wouldn't scare them all away! To catch the animals, the hunters chased them off cliffs or encircled them in fire, then shot them.

Buckskin

Softened, smoke-treated rawhide. Used by Kansas Indians to make clothes, bags and pouches.

Bow

Made from wood, horn or bone. Kansas Indian children learned how to use bows. The bowstring was made from animal gut, rawhide or twisted vegetable fibers.

Bone

Animal bones were used by Kansas Indians to make buttons, whistles and other items.

Beads

Made of wood, shells, claws, minerals, seeds — you name it! Later, the Kansas Indians traded with white men for glass beads, used in some of their decorative arts.

C is for . . .

Charles Curtis

Born at what is now North Topeka in 1860; part Kaw who was a lawyer and politician. First Vice President of Indian descent. Served 8 terms in the U.S. House, and 20 years in the Senate. Vice President under Herbert Hoover from 1929-1933.

Chief

Leader of a tribe. Different titles meant different things. Some members were made chief because they owned deeds to land. Chieftainship was often inherited, usually from the mother!

Contact Period

What historians call the era in the 1500s when Native Americans first met Europeans. This meeting changed the lifestyle of the Kansas Indians more than anyone could ever have anticipated!

Comanche

Famous Indian tribe of the Plains. Expert horsemen. Famous horse breeders and trainers with huge herds. Buffalo hunters and warlike. Migrated to present-day Kansas by 1719. Roamed much of the Plains in the 1700 and 1800s. It has been estimated that the Comanche killed more non-Indians per tribe member than any other tribe. These fierce warriors kept the Spanish from developing much of the lower plains. Eventually forced to live on a reservation in Oklahoma.

Confederacy

A union of different groups of people. A confederacy in Indian culture was a group of tribes that agreed not to fight with each other. They agreed to live peacefully. Sometimes the tribes shared culture and language.

Cheyenne

Important plains Indians; nomadic hunters after acquiring the horse in the late 1700s. Chief Dull Knife, with a small band of Indians, fought their way through Kansas, temporarily escaping American soldiers and forced removal to a reservation.

Citizenship

The Indian Citizenship Act of 1924 states all Indians born in the United States are citizens of the United States, and citizens of the states they live in, even though they may live on a reservation. They can vote. They pay most local, state and federal taxes, including sales taxes.

Council Grove

Site in east-central Kansas where U.S. government commissioners and Osage chieftains met in 1825. Signed a treaty guaranteeing peaceful travel along the Santa Fe Trail through Kansas.

Clan

A tribal unit. Members are descended from the same ancestor.

Canoe

The Indians invented this useful boat. The "rough" side of the canoe was on the outside, not the inside!

D is for . . .

Dance

There were Indian dances for every occasion: war, peace, hunting, rain, good harvests, etc. Drums, rattles, and flutes of bone or reed provided the music. Dancers often chanted or sang while performing. Steps were not easy to learn and required consistent practice.

Descendants

The first Kansas Indians were descendants of primitive hunters who crossed the Bering Strait from Asia to what is now Alaska. At that time, glacial ice still covered most of North America. These people were the true discoverers of the "New World!"

Disease

Kansas Indians had no immunity to the diseases that white explorers, colonists and settlers brought to their lands. These diseases included smallpox, measles, tuberculosis and others, which ravaged the tribes in great epidemics that killed many, and sometimes all, members of a tribe.

Delaware Indians

What the Lenni Lenape were called historically. In 1835 most of this once important Indian tribe were gathered on a reservation in Kansas. You can still find them there today, known as the Delaware-Muncie Tribe, located in Pomono, Kansas.

Dyes

Made of lichens, berries, roots, bark, plants, and other natural materials by Indians in Kansas. Different colors were used depending on what materials were available and what objects were to be dyed.

Dwellings

The Wichita Indians lived in villages of unique houses. They were pole-framed and grass-thatched, partly domed, but more conical at the top. They looked like giant haystacks!

Dishes

Made from clay, bark, wood, stone, and other materials, depending on what was available and what food they would be used for.

Dreams

Important in the Indian tradition. It was believed that dreams were the "windows" to the soul. Many thought a person's hidden desires were expressed in dreams.

E is for . . .

Eagle

An animal used in many Indian ceremonies. Eagle feathers attached to war bonnets and shields communicated an Indian's rank in his tribe and what kinds of deeds he had done. Feathers also adorned rattles, pipes, baskets, and prayer sticks.

El Cuartelejo

The remnants of an unusual stone and adobe dwelling of the Picuris Indians still stands in Scott County.

Early Encounters

When French explorers, Jacques Marquette and Louis Jolliet, came to our area in 1673, to explore the Mississippi River, they encountered Osage and Pawnee Indians. American explorers, Meriwether Lewis and William Clark," passed Kansa (Kaw) villages on the Missouri River when they came through Kansas in 1804.

El Turco

Pawnee Indian who acted as a guide to the explorer Coronado, but in reality, led him on a wild-goose chase through Kansas!

Earrings

Medicine men sometimes pierced male and female ears at special ceremonies. Earrings, which cost parents or relatives a significant amount, symbolized wealth and distinction. The more earrings that an Indian wore, the greater his honor. Some earrings measured 12 inches in length!

Environment

Preserving the environment is important to preserving Native American heritage. For thousands of years, Native American tribes lived completely off the land. Farming, mining, pollution have all had a part in changing native environments.

English

In the 1800s, the U.S. government built boarding schools for Indian children throughout the nation. Children were forced to leave their homes and families to live at these schools. They were required to learn English and not speak their native languages.

Epidemics

Few Indians possessed immunity to the deadly diseases, like smallpox and measles, which European explorers and settlers brought to the New World. As a result, great population loss took place. Sometimes entire tribes became extinct. Epidemics sparked by Hernando De Soto's expedition are estimated to have killed 75% of the native population in the New World.

F is for . . .

Fetish

These small objects were thought to hold the spirit of an animal or a part of nature. A fetish could be an object found in nature, such as bone or wood, or it could be a carved object. The fetish was usually small enough to be carried in a small bag or on a cord. The making and use of a fetish was kept secret by its owner and only shared with the one who inherited it.

Fox

This was a seminomadic Great Lakes tribe. Had three kinds of leaders—the peace chief, the war chief, and the ceremonial leader. Formed an alliance with the Sac in 1734 that continues today. Pressured into selling their lands and moving to Kansas in 1842.

Fur Trading

Indian trappers could sell glossy beaver pelts for as much as $8.00 in gold to whites back in Missouri, or trade them for cloth, flour, whiskey and rifles.

Fire Drill

A device used by Indians to make fires which consisted of a stick and a piece of wood with a tight hole in it. The stick was twirled rapidly in the hole, creating friction that would ignite shredded grass or wood powder placed nearby to start a fire.

Farmers

Many Kansas Indians, ancient and modern, have farming ways! Even pre-contact Indians tilled and irrigated, raising many important crops. Corn, cotton, beans, squash, melons, sunflowers, gourds, pumpkins and tobacco are all native Indian crops!

Federal Recognition

The United States government's official acknowledgement of a group of Indians as a tribe that is eligible for government benefits, programs and funds.

Footwear

Kansas Indians wore different footwear depending on their tribe and environment. Moccasins were made mostly of animal skin. Sandals were made of rawhide or plant material.

First on the Land

When Spanish explorers first reached Kansas, the tribes living here included the Kansa (or Kaw), Osage, Wichita, Pawnee and Picuris. Indian reservations in Kansas today include the Iowa Reservation at White Cloud, Kickapoo Reservation at Horton, Prairie Band Potawatomi Reservation at Mayetta and the Sac and Fox Reservation at Reserve. The Delaware-Muncie, the United Tribe of Shawnee, and the Swan Creek and Black River Chippewa are also represented in our state.

G is for . . .

Gens

Group of related members from different tribes.

Games

Adults played ball and other games of chance or skill. Indian children spun tops, fought pretend battles, did target-shooting, walked on stilts, played hide and seek, or competed to see who could hold their breath the longest!

Gathering

Native Americans gathered natural materials for food, fuel, baskets, clothing, and housing. American Indians tribes also hunted to meet basic needs. Even though some tribes planted crops, most did some kind of gathering.

Gorgets

Beautiful ornaments hung around the neck or from ears; their significance, if any, is unknown.

Gourds

Hollowed-out shell of a gourd plant's dried fruit which often grew into a specific shape. Indians raised many species of gourds. They were used for spoons, bowls, masks, rattles, and even storage.

Go To These Exciting Indian Events in Our State

All Nations Native American Center Pow Wow – April, Arkansas City; Haskell Indian Nations University Pow-wow & Commencement Celebration – May, Lawrence; Annual Prairie Band Potawatomi Nation Pow Wow – June, Mayetta; Kaw Nation Powwow, June, Council Grove; Annual Inter-Tribal PowWow Shawnee County – August, Topeka; Coffeyville Intertribal Powwow & Art Market – November, Coffeyville; Kickapoo Pow-Wow – September, Horton.

H is for . . .

Horn and Hooves

Indians used animal horn to make spoons and dishes. Hooves were made into rattles and bird beaks were used for decoration.

Hatchet

A small, short-handled ax, primarily used as a tool, not as a weapon. When settlers moved in, stone hatchets were replaced with iron ones.

Hair

Indians used hair as a textile. Hair from bison, mountain sheep, elk, moose, deer, dog, rabbit, beaver, or even humans were used to weave cloth, make wigs, or stuff pillows, balls, dolls or drumsticks.

Horses

Spaniards brought the horse to America. At first, Indians were afraid of the horse or thought it was sacred. Later, Indians "broke" horses gently, often "hypnotizing" them with a blanket. Horses were used for trade, barter or payment. Some Indians ate horse meat in hopes of gaining the animal's power. After getting the horse, Comanche, Kiowa, Cheyenne and Arapaho Indians pushed into western Kansas in the 1800s, because they were able to travel farther distances.

Hunters

Early Indian peoples were hunters who used wooden spears with stone points to kill many kinds of large mammals that are extinct today, such as mammoths and mastodons!

Huron

These Indians were powerful Great Lakes traders. Iroquois invasions scattered the Huron and caused a series on migrations to the U.S. side of the lakes in the late 1600s. Their native name, Wyandot, used when talking about tribal members who relocated to the U.S. The name Huron is used when referring to these Indians in Canada. By 1842, they had sold their lands and were moved to Wyandotte County, Kansas, in Indian Territory. Their final relocation was from there to Oklahoma.

Hairstyle

The hairstyle of the Pawnee was very distinctive. It was an upright and curved scalplock hairstyle. In fact, the Pawnee name probably comes from the Caddoan word "pariki," meaning "horn."

I is for . . .

Indian Country

Historic term referring to land beyond the frontier, that at one time included Kansas and other states. Later used as another name for the place the U.S. government settled the Indians from eastern America that were forced to relocate from their native lands. Many Indians died on their way to Kansas from exposure to the weather, poor nutrition, disease, and poor treatment from whites.

Indian Removal Act of 1830

This federal act gave President Andrew Jackson the power to relocate tribes east of the Mississippi to an "Indian Territory." The forced removal of the southeast Indians later became known as the "Trail of Tears."

Indian Territory

After treaties promised Kansas Indians that they would retain their lands here "forever," the U.S. government took the lands away, forcing the Indians onto smaller pieces since the area was designated as Indian Territory. Originally Indian Territory included all of Kansas, most of Oklahoma, and parts of Nebraska, Colorado and Wyoming. Never made official by Congress, Indians were removed to the Territory anyway. The Territory got smaller and smaller over 40 years, until only an area the size of Oklahoma without the panhandle remained.

Independence

Native American tribes are sovereign nations. That means they are independent. Some even issue their own passports! However, Native Americans are also considered citizens of the United States and enjoy all the rights and privileges of U.S. citizens.

Indian

In 1493, Christopher Columbus called the native people he met in North America "Indians" because he mistakenly believed he had sailed to India! Today, this term includes the aborigines of North and South America.

Indian Ladder

Indians made ladders by trimming branches off a tree. Some were left at consistent intervals to provide steps.

Indian Tribes in Kansas

At one time or another, these tribes have lived in the state of Kansas:

Apache, Comanche, Fox, Huron (Wyandot), Kaw, Kickapoo, Kiowa, Lenni Lenape, Miami, Nez Perce, Osage, Otoe, Ottawa, Pawnee, Potawatomi, Sac, Shawnee, Wichita.

J is for . . .

Just So You Know . . .

Today you can find many Kansas Indians that follow some traditional ways. But there are also many who are entrepreneurs, doctors, lawyers, educators and even politicians! If you visit a reservation or cultural event, make sure you know visitor etiquette. Often dances are religious ceremonies and should be observed as such; religious dances should not be applauded. Photography, videotaping and drawing are all important issues - check with the tribe or individual before any is started.

Justice

For hundreds of years, Native Americans have not received justice from federal and state governments. Native Americans have had nearly all their land taken away. Native Americans still have to fight for their rights in courts across the land.

Jacal

A house built from adobe and wood.

Judicial Termination

Modern term to describe current efforts by various U.S. government agencies and officials (especially the judicial system) to legally decrease the sovereignty of independent Indian tribes.

Jerked Meat

Thin strips of buffalo, elk, deer or other animal meat which is dried on racks in the sun; also called "jerky."

Just In Time!

The Indian Arts and Crafts Act of 1990 makes it against the law to pretend that an item has been made by Native Americans if it is really not. It is illegal to offer or display for sale, or sell any art or craft product in a way that falsely suggests it is Indian produced.

K is for . . .

Kickapoo

Tribe that migrated to Kansas from the southern Great Lakes in the mid 1800s. Allied with the Sac and Fox from early history. Some fought in the Black Hawk War of 1832. You can find their descendants on the Kickapoo Reservation in Horton.

Kiowa

Warlike Indian tribe who were horse Indians and buffalo hunters. Among the most fierce warriors of America's Indians. In the early 1700s, the Kiowa settled along the Cimarron River.

Knife

Made from various materials such as bone, reed, stone, wood, antler, shell, metal, or animal teeth (bear, beaver, etc.), knives were used as weapons but also creative handiwork.

Kansas

State named for the Kansa (also known as the Kaw) Indians; name means "South Wind."

Kaw

This tribe was also known as the Kansas, and is where the name of our state comes from. Their homelands were along the Kansas River. The Santa Fe Trail ran through their territory. Due to their distinct hairstyle of a shaved head with a single lock at the back, they were easily recognizable. Their lands were reduced, exchanged and then almost all was lost to the relocation of other tribes, settlement, and allotment.

Keokuk

Sac (Sauk) Indian leader who died in Kansas in 1848. Admired by Americans for his wisdom and gift of speech.

L is for . . .

Linguistic Families

There are 56 related groups of American Indian languages. A few of these speech families include Iroquoian, Algonquian, Siouan, Muskogean, Athapascan, and Wakashan.

Leggings

Both men and women wore cloth or skin covering, which were often decorated with quills, beads, or painted designs, for their legs.

Lost Tribes of Israel

This historic theory has been floating around since 721 BC. The 10 lost tribes of Israel are supposedly groups of people gathered together by Sargon, the King of Assyria. Some say he cast out 10 of the 12 tribes of Israel. Many have tried to prove that the American Indians are these missing tribes!

Lodge

The term for a type of Indian house that was usually a permanent dwelling. The population of a tribe was often estimated by its number of lodges.

Lenni Lenape

What the Delaware Indians called themselves; means "real men.". Forced to give up lands many times. Lived in at least 10 different states and signed 45 different treaties, often believing they were leasing the land. They sold Manhattan island, signed the Penn treaties, and were the first tribe to sign a treaty with the U.S.!

Lance

Spear used for hunting and war. The hunting lance had a short shaft and a broad, heavy head. The war lance was light and had a long shaft.

Lariat

These throw ropes made of rawhide, buffalo hair, or horsehair sometimes measured up to 20 feet long!

Land Loss

Native Americans lost their land in many ways. Conflicts with other tribes, colonization, European settlement, treaties, and removal took away Indian lands.

M is for . . .

Mortar and Pestle

A two-part milling tool, with a bowl-shaped stone, plus a club-shaped stone (or wooden bowl and wooden club), used for pulverizing or grinding plants or animal matter.

Masks

A face covering made from wood, basketwork, pottery or hides. Carved, painted and decorated with shells, fiber, hair, or feathers. Each mask had a special meaning.

Maize

Also called Indian Corn. Known as a "cereal" plant because it probably began as some form of grass. The Indians in our state figured out every possible way to use corn as a food. The only thing the white man added was the creation of "corn flakes!"

Medicine

Medicine could be good or bad. Medicines or charms were placed in a bag by young warriors and carried at all times. Some of the roots, leaves and bark that Indians in our state used as medicine are being rediscovered and used by today's doctors!

Moccasins

Indian shoes made of animal skin.

Medicine Man

A person who got the power to heal the sick through a secret means, usually from a dream or visions.

Miami

Indian tribe that came to Kansas in 1827. A combination of woodland and prairie style Indians. The made dugouts from single trees. To kill buffalo, they set fire to grass on 3 sides of a herd and shot the animals when they rushed out the open side to escape. Main tribe involved in Little Turtle's War. About half of the Miami were relocated to Kansas in 1846. In the 1860s, due to white settlement, they were relocated again to Oklahoma.

N is for . . .

Nomadic

A way of life in which people frequently moved from one location to another in search of food. "Seminomadic" people had permanent villages, but left them in certain seasons to hunt, fish, or gather wild plant foods. Many Kansas Indians preferred to move around, following the migrating buffalo than to settle down in established villages.

Needle

The kind of needle we think of for sewing was very rare among the Indians. They did have some needles made from bone, wood, cactus spines and the locust tree. The iron needle was brought over with the settlers. Thread used included horsehair, human hair and plant fibers.

Nation

There are many Indian nations located within the United States, such as the Kaw Nation. Indian nations are called nations because their governments and laws are independent of and separate from the U.S. government. The federal government must have "government to government" relations with these Indian nations, just as it would with foreign nations, like England or Spain.

November

In 1990, President George Bush approved a joint resolution designating November 1990 "National American Indian Heritage Month." Similar proclamations have been issued each year since 1994.

Names

Indian names were often changed during one's lifetime. These names could be derived from events that happened during the person's birth, childhood, adolescence, war service, or retirement from active tribal life. Some names came from dreams, some were inherited, and sometimes names were stolen or taken in revenge. Today some Indians maintain old, traditional Indian names, while others take modern names. Since settlers often did not read or write Indian languages, they recorded Indian names phonetically (as they "sounded"). Thus Indian names were often misspelled.

Nez Perce

Merchants and warriors whose ancestral territory was in the Northwest. Known for their breeding of strong, swift horses. Name means "pierced nose," but only a few actually did this. Following Chief Joseph's flight during the Nez Perce War, he and his people were sent to Kansas, and then to Indian Territory, before being sent back to a reservation in Washington state.

National Museum of the American Indian

The Smithsonian's National Museum of the American Indian on the National Mall in Washington, D.C., symbolizes a deeper understanding between America's first citizens and those who have come to make these shores their home.

O is for . . .

Osage

Part of the original Osage territory was in southeastern Kansas. They could be found along the Arkansas River. A seminomadic tribe, they hunted buffalo and farmed. Each village had a war chief and a peace chief, and their villages were divided into a northern section for the peace chief's people, and a southern section for the war chief's people. Gave up their lands between 1808 and 1865, for a reservation in Oklahoma.

Ottawa

Noted traders originally from the Great Lakes area. A group living in agreed to exchange their Michigan lands for ones in Kansas in 1831. In 1867 they were relocated to Indian Territory.

Origins

Some scientists believe that Native Americans actually came across a land bridge between Asia and North America. They say that during an ice age thousands of years ago, the water level was much lower and people could have walked between the two continents.

Otoe

This tribe, kinsmen to the Ioway, once had temporary villages in Kansas. Pressured to give up their lands, and the piece they were given no good, the Otoe received land in Kansas in 1854. Later it was all sold, and they relocated to Indian Territory.

Oil

Indians extracted oil from the many layers of fat that came with fresh bear meat. The fat was boiled down in earthen pots to produce the oil, which was stored in gourds and pots. The oil was used for cooking and even beautifying the body! Indians would mix red pigment with the oil, add the fragrances of cinnamon and sassafras, and rub it all over their bodies.

Orators

Many Indian leaders were excellent public speakers. Powerful and dramatic speakers were vital to leaders who wanted to influence their tribe. Watch for famous Indian quotations in literature and textbooks!

Office of Indian Education Programs

This is a service organization devoted to providing quality education opportunities for American Indian people. Established in the latter part of the nineteenth century to carry out the federal government's education commitment to Indian tribes, it has become the only national education system for American Indian children and adults.

P is for . . .

Powwow

The original form of the word meant "medicine man." Medicine men would often use noise motion and confusion to scare away harmful spirits and cure people. It was also a gathering to talk about political matters. Today, the powwow is an event where Indians gather to sing, perform ceremonial dances, and share cultural pride and traditions.

Potawatomi

Their ancestral lands were in the Great Lakes region. A series of migrations due to poverty and hardship moved them in a southwestern direction. Some migrated to several other states before coming to Kansas; others went directly to Kansas, where a band remains today.

Pawnee

Among the first Indians to live on the plains. They were peaceful friends and allies of white settlers. They hunted and gathered, by were also highly skilled farmers that were seminomadic. They were the most famous of all the U.S. Army Indian Scouts. Their ancestral lands in southern Kansas were lost in the mid 1800s.

Paint

Indians used many natural materials to make paint, like clay mixed with oil or grease. Yellow "paint" was made with the gall bladder of a buffalo! Why did they paint their faces or bodies? Indians used paint to look scary or beautiful, to disguise themselves, or to protect their skin from sunburn or insect bites. Indians often applied red paint because it symbolized strength and success.

Picuris Indians

Once lived in western Kansas.

Pemmican

Indian food made of animal meat, which was dried in the sun, pounded together with fat and berries. The mixture was packed into skin bags and used primarily while on the trail.

Papoose

An American Indian infant aged between birth and one year is called a papoose. A papoose spent most of his or her days snugly wrapped in a kind of cradle made of skins or bark and a wooden frame that hung on the mother's back. This sturdy frame also allowed a mother to lean her papoose against a tree or rock within sight as she worked.

Picture History

Some Indians kept a record of time and important events by painting or drawing pictures or symbols on skin, bark, or stone.

Pottery

Indian pottery was made from built-up spirals of clay that were molded or paddled, or a combination of the two methods. Most pottery served as cooking vessels.

Q is for . . .

Quillwork

Indians used the quills of porcupine or birds to make a type of embroidery. Quills were dyed with juice from berries and other materials. When they were ready to be used, the quills were either mashed with teeth or softened with hot water and flattened with rocks. The quills were then laced into moccasins, shirts, pipe covers, and other items. Beads which Indians received by trading with settlers eventually replaced quillwork.

Quality

Native American arts and crafts are known for their excellent craftsmanship and striking designs. This work is often influenced by things found in nature especially plants and animals.

Quiver

Case used to hold arrows; made of woven plant materials or animal skins.

Quivira

What an Indian slave called a kingdom that supposedly had streets paved of gold. Belief in this legend brought Spanish explorers to the Kansas area around 1540 in search of riches. Also the name of the Wichita Indians.

Quirt

A short riding whip with a wood, bone, or horn handle.

R is for . . .

Rain Dancing

The rain dance ceremony, performed to encourage rainfall, was common among Indian religions because good weather is vital for a successful harvest. Rainmakers were in tune with nature; there are actual reported cases of Indians producing or preventing rain!

Roots

Indians used plant roots for food, medicine, dye, baskets, cloth, rope, salt, flavoring, and just to chew!

Rattles

Indians of Kansas made rattles from bird beaks, animal hooves, bones, pods, seashells, turtle shells and other animal parts. The rattles are used in ceremonies.

Rawhide

Untanned animal hide. The "green" hide was stretched on the ground or over a frame. Flesh and fat were removed. The skin was dried, washed, then buried with wood ashes which made the hair come off. Used by the Kansas Indian to make drumheads, lash lodge poles, mend broken objects and in many other ways.

Revered People

Amongst the Osage, there was a special group of highly respected men called the Little Old Men. This council of elderly tribe members made the tribal laws and settled disputes within the tribe.

Reservations

The U.S. government set aside, or "reserved," land for the Indians. These reservations originally served as a sort of prison during the beginning stages of Indian removal. At that time, reservations provided the government with some control over Indian activity and residency. This land was usually considerably less desirable land than the Indians' native territories. Today's reservations are lands that are tribally held, yet protected by the government.

Removal

The U.S. government policy of the 1830s-1850s that removed Indians from their native lands to new lands, primarily west of the Mississippi River.

S is for . . .

Sac

This tribe was also referred to as the Sauk. Seminomadic people originally from the Great Lakes region. After selling lands in Iowa, the Sac and their close allies the Fox, moved to Kansas when it was part of the Indian Territory. Descendants can be found today on their reservation in Reserve.

Sign Language

A way for Indians to communicate with others from a tribe whose language they did not speak.

Shaman

Medicine man and spiritual leader who was supposed to have special healing power from another world.

Shawnee

Although their ancestral territory seems to have been in Tennessee, the Shawnee split into different groups and migrated often. There were temporary villages throughout the Southeast, Mid-Atlantic and in the eastern Midwest. In the 1800s, Shawnee bands could be found living in the plains states, including Kansas.

Sweatlodge

Structure used for ritual purification by sweating from exposure to very hot fires or hot steam from pouring water over hot stones. Also called a sweathouse, for some tribes also doubling as clubhouses.

Stone-boiling

Cooking method by placing preheated stones into cooking vessels.

Sacred Bundles

A group of objects treasured by a tribe. They were well-guarded and often taken into battle. The items were publicly shown only on very important occasions.

Saddle

While some Indians did use saddles on their horses, most rode bareback!

Southern Sioux

A tern used to refer to Siouan-speaking Indian tribes which included the Iowa, Kansa, Missouri, Omaha, Osage, Otoe and Ponca. Not to be confused with the Sioux Indians! They were buffalo-hunters and farmers. Most lived in villages and used tepees when on the trail for a hunt.

Signals

Indian signs made with a pony, blanket, mirror, smoke, fire-arrow or other item to communicate over long distances.

Sachem

The supreme Indian ruler of an area where there are many related tribes.

T is for . . .

Tobacco
A sacred plant early Indians used to make offering to their gods, cure diseases, bring good luck, seal agreements and bind treaties.

Treaties
Written agreements between the U. S. government and the Indians, most of which involved the Indians giving up their native lands.

Throwing Stick
A sling or grooved stick used to hurl a lance or spear. It was used by Kansas Indians before bows and arrows.

Totem
The spirit of some natural object (usually an animal) taken by an Indian, tribe or family to guard over them.

Topeka
Indian name for a potato-like root that once grew near the present-day Kansas city of the same name.

Tomahawk
A club, axe or hammer used to chop wood, drive stakes in the ground or as a weapon.

Tracking
To follow a trail by finding a sign such as a broken blade of grass, a moved stone or moccasin track. Indians learned to trail as children, so that they could find food, track enemies and disguise their own signs.

Teeth
Kansas Indians hung teeth on cords to make necklaces.

Trail of Death
This is the name for the migration of the Potawatomi that began in the fall 1838. Many of the tribe lost their lives to disease and hunger along the way. Over 800 Potawatomi in Indiana were rounded up at Twin Lakes and marched all the way across Illinois and Missouri to Osawatomi, Kansas. Today, the Trail of Death has been declared a Regional Historic Trail.

Tribe
A group of Indians with shared culture, history, original territory, ancestry, social organization, and governmental structure. A tribe may contain several bands of Indians.

Thunderbird
A mythological Indian figure, as well as a part of the constellations for many Indians. Thunderbird mythology is mostly different from tribe to tribe, in general either coexisting with ancestors as an actual bird, or appearing as a spiritual nature god. The Thunderbird was good to the people in either case. Much mythology ties the thunderbird with thunder, lightning and storms.

U is for . . .

U.S. Bureau of Indian Affairs

Provides public services such as law enforcement, land records, economic development, and education to Indians. Known for mismanagement and ethical problems.

U.S. Army

Many Native Americans have fought bravely for the United States Army. Many have also given their lives for a country that was not always accepting of them.

Unique

Each and every tribe has its own unique customs, language, and traditions.

U.S. Indian Schools

The Bureau of Indian Affairs operates hundreds of federal schools around the nation. Enrollment of Native American children measures in the thousands!

U.S. Indian Reorganization Act

Passed by Congress in 1934, the act authorized Indian tribes to establish and conduct their own governments, and to form businesses.

U.S. Colonists

Called Long Knives or Big Knives by early Indians, who also called English explorers "Coat Men."

U.S. President

Once called Great White Father by Indians.

U.S. Indian Wars

The U.S. War Department has compiled an official list of "Indian Wars" that occurred in the United States. Over 50 wars were fought between the U.S. and the Indians during the period of 1790-1850.

V is for . . .

Vessels

Indians carried water in special gourds shaped liked bottles, called water vessels.

Village Councils

These were held in the town (council) house and occurred to discuss and decide important matters. Harmony and agreement was essential to tribal unity. Rather than vote on issues, they were discussed until everyone was satisfied. Anyone who wanted to could speak freely. Everyone did not always agree on the outcome, but everyone avoided conflict by pushing their case.

Vegetable Dyes

Indians could not buy color from the store like we can today. Instead, they created many different colors from the things they found on earth like plants, flowers, shrubs, trees, roots, and berries. They made beautiful and unique reds, oranges, yellows, greens, browns, and violets. These dyes were used for baskets, pottery, weaving, body makeup, and clothing.

Very Hungry

There were Indians who here hunters, gatherers and foragers, that often ate whatever they could find! How hungry would you have to be to eat what they sometimes ate: reptiles, larvae, and insects?

Villages

Many Kansas Indians lived in villages! Villages were formed around different clans or bands within the tribe, but could also contain different clans living together. Villages were usually permanent settlements, although semi-nomadic tribes have been known to migrate between permanent villages.

Vesperic Indians

Indian tribes located in the United States.

W is for . . .

War Bonnet

Special headdress worn into battle, often adorned with feathers.

War Pony

Horse, often painted with colorful paint and ridden into battle.

Women

Indian women in some tribes were poor and hardworking, like the men. But in some tribes, women had many rights, including becoming chief!

Whistle

Indians from Virginia made them from the wing bones of birds. The whistles made the sound of the bird the bones came from! Used to communicate, signal, sound an alarm or even flirt with a maiden!

Wichita

Confederacy of 5 Caddoan groups that once lived in Kansas. Known for their haystack-like houses. Hunted buffalo, but also farmed. They tattooed themselves, and were important traders. Left Kansas in the late 1600s, but returned to the present-day Wichita area briefly in the 1860s.

Wohaw

What the Plains Indians of Kansas called the cow.

War Club

A weapon made of stone, bone, or wood in the shape of a club.

White Man

Indians generally called them Pale Face, a name the white men themselves suggested!

War Dance

Indian braves danced this before going into battle. The dance was a way of assembling the braves and getting them to commit to the fight ahead.

XYZ are for . . .

Xenophobe

A xenophobe is someone who is afraid of foreign people, their customs and cultures, or foreign things. Many of the first European settlers were afraid of Native American cultures.

You Bet!

Some Native Americans say that Casinos make a lot of money. Others say that too many people have a gambling problem. In the 1980s and 1990s, many tribes discussed whether or not gambling casinos should be allowed. Now that many casinos have been built across the country, the debate has switched to how it should be controlled.

Zounds!

Between 1871 and 1913, at least 98 traditional agreements between tribes and the United States were negotiated and 96 of them were ratified by Congress. Each agreement remains as law (unless changed by a later agreement)!

ZZZZZZ...

Shamans and medicine men were not the only people who had access to the spirit world. Indians believed that people could make contact with spirits every night in their dreams! Dreamers could travel back to the time of man's creation or far ahead into their own futures. They also believed that dreams contained warnings or commands from the spirits. Many tribes felt that they had to act out their dreams as soon as they awoke. If an Indian dreamed about bathing, for example, he would run to his neighbors' houses first thing in the morning, and his neighbors would throw kettles full of cold water over him.

Y... Or, "Why?"

1. Why do you think Indian warriors carried charms with them? Some Indian medicines have been scientifically proven to have true healing power and are still used today. Do you think their charms had any real power to help them win battles?
2. Why do you think the American government kept relocating Indians onto reservations and then making the reservations smaller and smaller?
3. Why did Indians use items such as a pipe in ceremonies? What kinds of symbolic objects do we use in ceremonies today?
4. Why and how did Indians use natural materials in creative ways?
5. Many Indian tribes are running successful businesses on their reservations today. There is one industry that many tribes are making a lot of money at. Do you know what this is? Hint: "I'll bet you do!"

Which Famous Native American Am I?

Solve the puzzle!

Word Bank

Black Elk	Crazy Horse	Sitting Bull	Sequoia
Sacajawea	Chief Joseph	Geronimo	Pocahontas

Down

1. This Shoshone woman joined Lewis and Clark as their guide and translator and helped make the expedition a success! Hint: She has 4 "a"s in her name!

4. This man gave the Cherokee their first alphabet so that they could write. Until then, they communicated only by speaking and drawing pictures. Hint: A famous ancient tree also has the same name!

5. He was one of the fiercest of Indian warriors! He fought against white settlers in Arizona and New Mexico to keep his people from being pushed off their lands. Hint: Jump!

Across

2. A legend says that this brave Algonquian woman saved the life of Englishman John Smith. Hint: Disney produced a movie about her.

3. He fought at Little Bighorn when he was only 13! He was also a wise "shaman" who saw visions and could advise people. Hint: Part of his name is an animal with antlers!

6. He was a great Sioux warrior who won the battle against General Custer at Little Bighorn in 1876. Hint: His horse was not crazy!

7. A leader of the Lakota (Sioux) tribe who lived on the Standing Rock Reservation in North Dakota after the battle of Little Bighorn. He tried to make conditions better for his people there, so the U.S. government called him a "troublemaker." Hint: He did not sit all the time!

8. A wise and brave chief of the Nez Percé who tried to bring his people to Canada to escape war. He said, "From where the sun now stands, I will fight no more forever." Hint: His father's name was "Old Joseph."

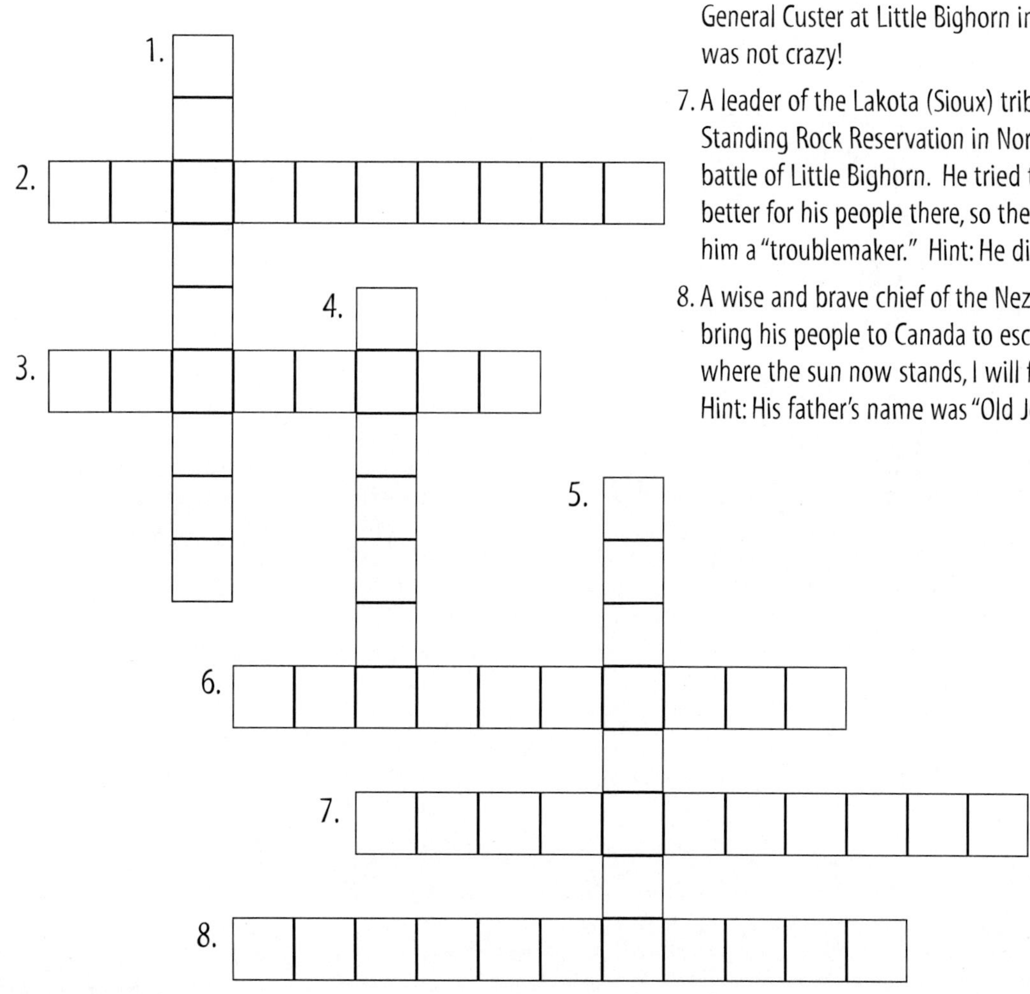

Answer Key: 1. Sacajawea; 2. Pocahontas; 3. Black Elk; 4. Sequoia; 5. Geronimo; 6. Crazy Horse; 7. Sitting Bull; 8. Chief Joseph

Different Ways for Different Indians!

North American Indian tribes are divided into different areas. In each of these areas, tribes shared common ways of living with each other. They might make similar arts or crafts, they might eat the same foods, or they might have had the same beliefs. These activities are all part of their "culture." Each area had its own culture, which was different from the tribes in all the other areas.

Below is a map of all the different groups of Indian tribes in North America. Color each area with a different color. You will see a colorful picture of how Native Americans can all be called "Indians" but still have very different cultures!

Celebration!

Powwows are big festivals where Native Americans gather to sing, dance, and eat together. It is a time to celebrate and show pride in their culture. Powwows can last from one afternoon to several days. The Indians dress in native costumes and dance ancient dances to the beating of drums.

Artists sell their arts and crafts. You might be able to buy some real Native American food cooked on an open fire. Native Americans go to powwows to be with each other, share ideas, and just have fun! Most powwows are also open to people who are not Indian. It's a great place to learn about Native American culture!

If you went to a powwow this weekend, what do you think you would see? What do you think might NOT be there? Circle the objects you think you would see at a powwow. Put an X through those you probably won't see.

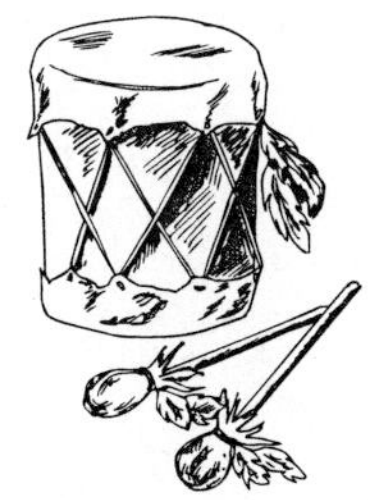

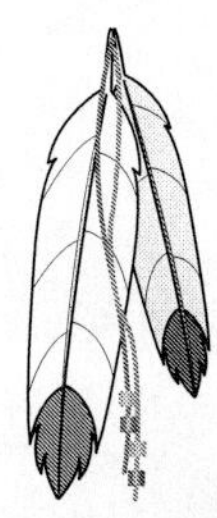

Answer Key: Circled objects are: beads, moccasins, open fire, drums, feathers, baskets, kids, food, drums, horse.

Make an Indian Weaving!

Many Native Americans used weaving to create useful things like sashes (belts), bags, mats, and blankets. They used animal hair to make yarn, and dyed the yarn with natural dyes from fruits and other plants. They also used some plant fibers, like cotton, to make weaving thread.

Weave a small Native American mat of your own. Use different colors of yarn to create a beautiful pattern in your weaving. Place a favorite object on the mat or hang it on your wall!

Prepare the "loom"

Cut a piece of cardboard 5 inches wide and 6 inches long. Along the two 5-inch sides (the "short" sides), have an adult cut slits 1/4 inch deep. These slits should be 1/2 inch apart from each other. So, on each short side you will have 9 slits.

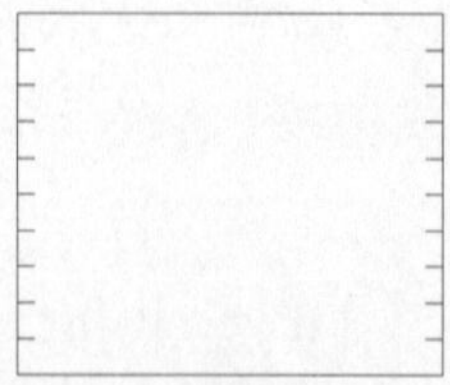

Directions:

1. Take a long piece of yarn and bring it from the back through the first slit (the one next to the edge of the cardboard.) The end of the yarn will hang down behind the cardboard.

2. Bring the yarn right across the front of the cardboard to the slit opposite the one your yarn came through.

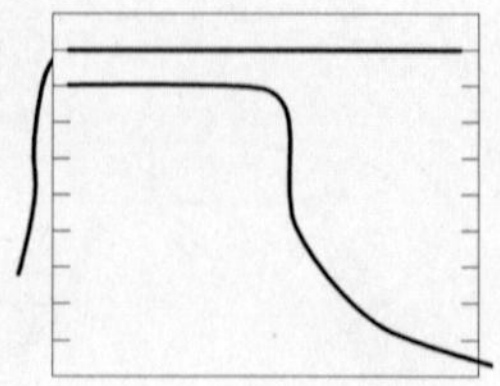

3. Now bring the yarn under the back of the cardboard and then up again through the second slit.

4. Repeat #2 and #3, until you have 9 strands of yarn across the front of your cardboard!

5. Then cut the yarn and tie the two loose ends in the back of the cardboard.

6. Take another piece of yarn and start feeding it through the 9 strands, going over one, under the next over the next, etc. When you get to the end, pull the yarn behind the cardboard and around to the front, and begin again. This time, whatever strand you went over, go under. And whatever strand you went under, go over.

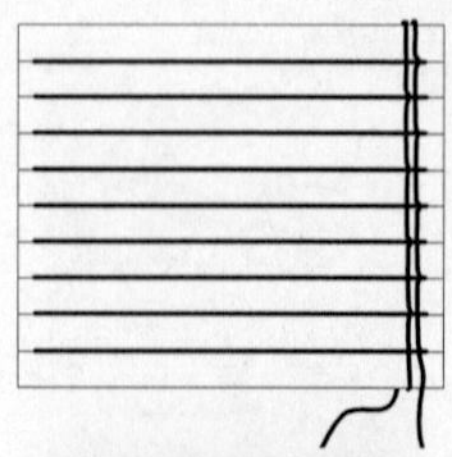

7. Repeat this pattern until the front of your cardboard in covered. Then cut the yarn in the back of the cardboard, and trim it to create a fringe for your mat!

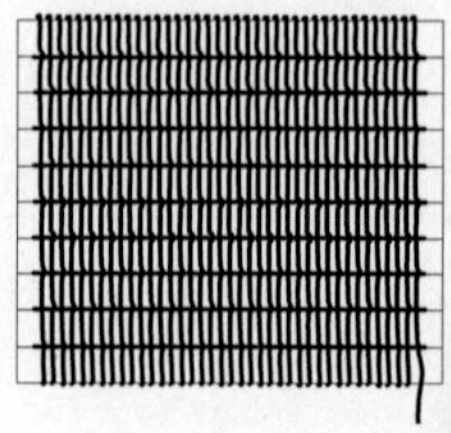

Tips:

- For a wild look, use variegated or different colored yarn!
- For a tighter mat, push the under/over strands up against the previous strands during weaving.
- To keep your mat from unravelling, tie neighboring fringe together up close to the mat.

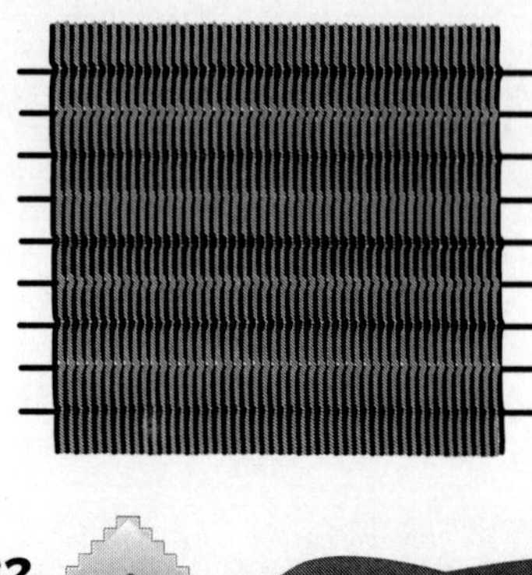

Finders Keepers?

Native Americans have many buried treasures. For hundreds of years, special objects would sometimes be buried with Native Americans, or maybe they would just be lost. Archeologists used to dig for interesting artifacts in old Native American gravesites. They would keep the Native American bones or the arrowheads, rattles, masks and other objects that they found. But this made the Native Americans feel like they were being robbed.

In 1990, the U.S. government passed a law that said that no one could look for or take these Native American objects anymore. And whoever had any already had to give them back to the people they belonged to. This is called repatriation

Help the archeologist return the artifact to a Native American.

Fast Fact

An artifact is an object that was made by people a long time ago for some useful purpose.

Busy Hands!

Before modern times, Native Americans didn't have stores where they went to buy things. They made everything they needed.

What did Indians make with their own hands? Use the Word Bank and pictures to find out!

Word Bank

blanket	moccasins	arrows	pottery	canoe
mat	food	jewelry	pouch	box

 ___ ___ ___

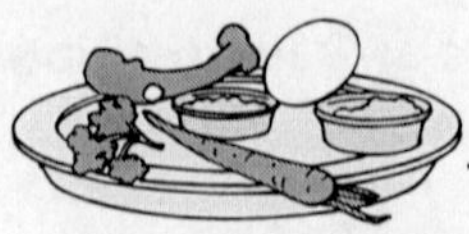 ___ ___ ___ ___

 ___ ___ ___

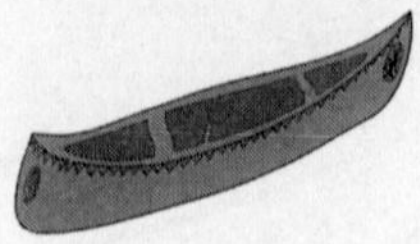 ___ ___ ___ ___ ___

 ___ ___ ___ ___ ___ ___ ___

 ___ ___ ___ ___ ___

 ___ ___ ___ ___ ___ ___ ___ ___ ___ ___

 ___ ___ ___ ___ ___ ___

 ___ ___ ___ ___ ___ ___ ___

 ___ ___ ___ ___ ___ ___ ___

American Indians Today

Beginning with the first letter of each group of letters, cross out every other letter to discover some new words. You may not have heard of these before, but you can read all about them!

1. Many Indians live on these, but many more do not!

TRYELSDEBRNVJAOTPIPOWNASX

____

2. Many Indians have been poor for a long time because for many years the government took away their lands and their ability to make a living.

TPKOOVWEBRNTXYA

____

3. Many Indians have been studying hard at school and going to college in order to earn more money. Education helps the Indians make their lives better. These Native Americans are working to become:

TSJUMCBCFEYSMSOFPUVL

____

4. This is a big term that means Native Americans have worked hard to get the U.S. government to let them rule themselves. This means that they have their own laws and make their own decisions. They are like a separate country inside the U.S.! Now, try and see if you can get your parents to give you the same thing!

TSGENLBF JDGEETSEWRAMCIHNUAKTYIKOTNU

______________ ______________________________

Fast Fact

What do Indians work as today?

- doctors
- nurses
- factory workers
- artists
- lawyers
- actors

The same kinds of jobs any American might work at!

Native Americans Move to the City!

Solve the code to discover the mystery words!

A	B	C	D	E	F	G	H	I	J	K	L	M
✳	❀	⌘	♣	➧	❤	❢	✯	✂	✆	☛	✈	✉
N	**O**	**P**	**Q**	**R**	**S**	**T**	**U**	**V**	**W**	**X**	**Y**	**Z**
✿	☆	✦	✡	✏	❥	☎	✒	✚	✖	✍	✠	✓

1. During the 1950s and 1960s, the American government paid Indians to leave their homes on reservations and move to cities to get jobs. If cities are sometimes called urban areas, then these brave Indians were called:

__ __ __ __ __   __ __ __ __ __ __ __

✒ ✏ ❀ ✳ ✿   ✂ ✿ ♣ ✂ ✳ ✿ ❥

2. Many Indians chose to stay on their reservations and not move to the city. They thought that if they moved to the city, they would lose the way of life that their parents and ancestors had taught. These Indians called themselves:

__ __ __ __ __ __ __ __ __ __ __   __ __ __ __ __ __ __

✏ ➧ ❥ ➧ ✏ ✚ ✳ ☎ ✂ ☆ ✿   ✂ ✿ ♣ ✂ ✳ ✿ ❥

3. Native Americans who moved to cities lived close to each other. They tried to keep their way of life as much as possible. They did not want to forget their religion, native art, or music. They did not want to lose their:

__ __ __ __ __ __ __

⌘ ✒ ✈ ☎ ✒ ✏ ➧

4. Are you afraid of heights? Many people are. The Mohawk Indians are not! Many of them work hundreds of feet above the city to build steel frames for skyscrapers. People who do this work above the city are:

__ __ __ __ __   __ __ __ __ __ __ __

❥ ☎ ➧ ➧ ✈   ✖ ☆ ✏ ☛ ➧ ✏ ❥

5. Today urban Indians and reservation Indians come together to celebrate their culture. They share ideas and stories. They dance and beat drums. They make and sell Indian jewelry. During these celebrations, Indians remember how much they have to be proud of! These big parties are called

__ __ __ __ __ __ __

✦ ☆ ✖ ✖ ☆ ✖ ❥